DIGGING UP THE PAST

by Francis Pryor
with David Collison

Reconstructions by Paul Birkbeck

B.T. Batsford Ltd · London

● Contents ●

Front Cover: The village of Cosmeston in South Wales was deserted in the fourteenth century, perhaps after the Black Death. The artist's reconstruction shows life there around 1300 AD.

First published 1993

Typeset by Deltatype Ltd, Ellesmere Port and printed in Hong Kong

Published by B.T. Batsford Ltd
4 Fitzhardinge Street, London W1H 0AH

A CIP catalogue record for this book is available from the British Library

ISBN 0 7134 7290 1

The late Tony Gregory, who presented Now Then I, was an archaeologist who specialized in prehistoric and Roman Britain. He also researched ways to make the past come to life.

Francis Pryor, who presented Now Then II, is an archaeologist who first discovered the famous Bronze Age remains at Flag Fen in Cambridgeshire. He now runs the Fenland Archaeological Trust and plays the concertina whenever he gets the chance.

Frontispiece: Past meets Present on the Isles of Orkney. In our TV series *Now Then*, two children played the part of children from the past – the *Time Children*, and two played the *Now Children*. Here, Sara Sheavills and James Shaw have appeared from the New Stone Age, or Neolithic – 5000 years ago. The Orkney *Now* children are Inga Cromarty, a farmer's daughter, and Roy Seatter, whose father is a lobster fisherman.

The three ages of man

Early in the last century a Danish archaeologist called C. J. Thomsen was trying to make sense of the Danish National Museum's collections of prehistoric objects. There was no writing in prehistoric times, so he had no way of knowing for sure which object was made first. He used his common sense and reasoned that it is easier to chip and polish a stone to make an axe, than to extract iron from ore in a furnace and beat it into shape while keeping it white-hot. The stone axe needs a few simple techniques and tools to make, whereas the iron axe requires control over fierce heat and other difficult skills. So he thought that it was likely that the stone axe was invented long before the iron axe. The Stone Age is therefore older than the Iron Age. In between the two he placed the Bronze Age, as bronze is a metal that is much simpler to make than iron. This system of placing things in their correct date order is known as the Three Age System, and it is still used by prehistorians.

Excavations at Cosmeston medieval village, Penarth, South Wales. The covering soil is gently trowelled and swept away to uncover what is beneath — a bit like rolling back the bedroom carpet and finding information underneath in the form of old newspapers!

A Saxon burial at West Heslerton, East Yorkshire.

What is archaeology?

Archaeology is the story of people and how they lived from the earliest times. Archaeologists try to discover as much as they can about ancient people, mainly using evidence that survives in the soil. This evidence is usually found in excavations. Excavations destroy the evidence at the same time as they discover it, so they have to be very carefully carried out. When an excavation is finished, the discoveries are published in books, or magazines.

Map showing the location of sites in the book.

TIME CHART

Dates (Approximate)	Archaeological period	Places and events described in this book
500,000–4500 BC	Old Stone Age (or Palaeolithic)	Hoyle's Mouth Cave
4500–1800 BC	New Stone Age (or Neolithic)	Orkney Islands sites Sites around Avebury
1800–700 BC	Bronze Age	Flag Fen
700 BC–AD 43	Iron Age	Maiden Castle
AD 43–410	Roman	Hadrian's Wall
AD 410–1066	Saxon	West Heslerton
AD 1066–1550	Medieval	Battle of Hastings Cosmeston medieval village Southampton merchant's house
AD 1550 –present	Post-Medieval	Kirby Hall Killhope lead mine

A summer's day, 13,000 years ago. Paul Birkbeck painted the Old Stone Age family living around Hoyle's Mouth Cave, near present-day Tenby in south-west Wales. When this family lived here in the Ice Age you could walk from Wales to Northern France.

A winter's day, 100 years ago. At the Killhope lead mines in County Durham, boys of nine and ten worked at the 'washing floor' breaking stones to extract the lead ore (see page 44).

When Hoyle's Mouth cave was occupied, herds of bison and wild horses roamed the grass-lands which are now covered by the waters of the Bristol Channel and the Irish Sea.

What is prehistory?

Prehistory is the story of people and things that existed before the invention of writing—this happened at different times in different places. In Britain writing (of the Latin language) was introduced by the Romans. So anything that happened in Britain before the Roman Conquest took place in prehistory.

The Old Stone Age

This is the oldest period of human prehistory. In Britain the earliest evidence for human activity comes from about half a million years ago. The Old Stone Age happened during the Ice Age. In actual fact the Ice Age was made up of several very cold periods that were separated by warmer times; today we are living in one of those warmer times, and it will probably become much colder in a few thousand years. The last Ice Age ended about 10,000 years ago.

Stone Age cave dwellers

Old Stone Age people lived in small groups—perhaps grandparents with their children and grandchildren. Sometimes, they chose to live in caves if a suitable one could be found, as the Ice Age climate outside could be very severe indeed. Mostly they lived in skin tents or other small structures which were probably warm and very weather-proof. They could not have survived in such severe conditions unless they had somewhere warm in which to eat and rest. Old Stone Age people knew how to make fire, and they would not have survived without this knowledge.

Hoyle's Mouth Cave

Limestone is a soft rock which is easily dissolved in water. Over the years, water flowing through or past layers of limestone carves natural caves. Hoyle's Mouth Cave is in limestone country near Carmarthen Bay in south-west Wales. Excavation has shown that this cave was occupied at least twice in the Old Stone Age. The first occupation took place around 30,000 years ago and the people who lived or stayed in the cave probably hunted a number of animals that are now extinct: such as the mammoth and the woolly rhinoceros. These animals were trapped in hidden pits dug by the hunters or were speared using flint-tipped spears.

The second occupation of Hoyle's Mouth Cave took place towards the end of the Old Stone Age, around 12,500 years ago. By this period the coldest weather had passed and there was a greater variety of smaller animals to hunt. If the number of known later Old Stone Age sites is anything to go by, the population of Britain was beginning to grow.

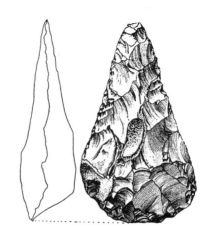

A flint axe from the Old Stone Age: about ⅓ life-size.

We think the people of the Old Stone Age must have made music. The Time Girl carries a bone flute, while her brother, armed with a flint-tipped spear, keeps guard.

LIFE AT THE END OF THE ICE AGE

The people at Hoyle's Mouth lived at a time when the great ice sheets that once covered large parts of northern Europe had retreated. The cold conditions came to an end about ten thousand years ago. Many of the animals that existed in Britain during the later Stone Age were very like the 'big game' that still survives in Africa: there were hairy elephants, such as the mammoth and the straight-tusked elephant (which both became extinct about 12,000 years ago); other animals included the woolly rhinoceros, the hippopotamus, bear, bison, musk ox, lion, wild dog and hyaena. The climate was not as hot as Africa, but these animals were adapted to it – after all, they survive perfectly well today in British zoos and safari parks.

In cold spells many of these animals moved south to warmer climates, but some (such as the woolly mammoth) were quite at home when it was very cold indeed. During warmer periods the Welsh countryside was cloaked in thick pine woodland, with fast-flowing mountain streams. These forests were first cleared by human communities about four to five thousand years ago.

What's this? Now Boy James Chiffi shows a 'find' to the archaeologist in charge of the excavation or 'dig'. It is often difficult to tell the difference between a man-made flint tool and a piece of chipped stone. The archaeologist knows the signs to look for.

The Neolithic – a revolution

The New Stone Age, or Neolithic period, was far more than just a more modern version of the Old Stone Age. The Neolithic was the period when the people of Britain and Europe learned how to produce their own food, by farming. Before the Neolithic, everyone's food came from hunting, fishing and from gathering wild plant foods, such as nuts, fruits, edible roots and berries. People did not go hungry because they knew how to use all the foods in the countryside, and when one source of food failed (due to disease or bad weather) another would take its place. The problem with this 'hunting and gathering' way of life is that wild foods are quite scarce and so only a very few people can live in any single part of the country. Farmed land, on the other hand, produces large amounts of food in quite a small area. This means that today food produced in the country can feed huge populations of people living in towns. Without farming there can be no towns, no industry, and no modern life. We owe a lot to those Neolithic farmers!

The first farmers in Britain

The idea of growing plants, or keeping tame animals for food was invented in several places across the world, and at various times. The invention of farming that concerns Europeans was one of the earliest, and it took place in the Middle East (in the modern countries of Iran and Iraq) in an area rich in wild grasses which were the ancestors of modern cereal crops, such as wheat and barley. As the idea of farming spread, it became more complicated and animals were also kept. Farming reached Europe (Greece) around 6500 BC and Britain around 4500 BC. But the sort of farming that happened in

---

The bull-roarer. This painting by Paul Birkbeck imagines a priest or witch-doctor summoning the spirits of dead ancestors inside the great chamber tomb at Maes Howe. A whirling wooden blade called a bull-roarer makes an eerie noise.

Neolithic Britain was very different from that of Greece which is far hotter and drier. In Britain the first farmers relied heavily on animals, such as cattle, sheep and pigs, and they also continued to hunt and fish.

Colin Richards' excavation at Barnhouse (left) clearly shows the foundations of a great circular building. The reconstruction (right) suggests a huge ritual-house, where important ceremonies took place in the New Stone Age, 5000 years ago.

Highlands and Islands

Archaeological sites are usually best preserved in the remoter parts of Britain, in the highlands and islands. In these areas there are fewer motorways, cities or farmers with powerful machines to destroy the remains of the past. But recently the planting of huge pine forests in Scotland and Wales, and in Ireland the digging of peat to fuel power stations has meant that archaeological sites in even the remotest places are at risk.

The Orkney Islands

Orkney, off the north-east of Scotland, is probably the most archaeologically exciting area in Britain. It is too windy for trees to grow easily, but the local stone splits naturally into evenly-shaped building blocks, so nearly all building was done in stone — and this has survived extremely well.

DISCOVERING ANCIENT SITES: FIELDWALKING

Archaeologists are very good at discovering new sites. The two most common methods are fieldwalking and air photography (which will be discussed later). Fieldwalking, as its name suggests, involves walking up and down a bare field and looking closely at the ground. Ploughing brings buried objects to the surface and the archaeologist knows what to look for. The archaeologist Colin Richards was fieldwalking in the Scottish island of Orkney when he discovered small pieces of broken pottery which he recognized at once as Neolithic. There was a lot of this pottery lying on the surface, but he was the first person to realize what it was and why it was important. We now know that the pottery came from a very well preserved Neolithic farmhouse hidden below the surface, at a place called Barnhouse.

Reconstruction of the settlement at Barnhouse, Orkney, with the stone circle of Stenness beyond.

Barnhouse

The Neolithic village at Barnhouse is immediately next to the Stones of Stenness (discussed below), and was built at the same time – five thousand years ago. It was probably missed by archaeologists in the past, who were too busy looking at the great Stenness stones, and was only discovered very recently by Colin Richards. His excavations have revealed the remains of stone-built round houses and a very large oval building which was surrounded by a stone wall. This main building was used for special occasions, when people died, or when a young man or woman became an adult. The Barnhouse buildings have fireplaces and stone-built 'dressers' which were more probably a combination of cupboard and household altar where valuable objects and things important to each family's history were kept.

Skara Brae

At Skara Brae is the most famous Neolithic 'house' in Europe. It consists of several roughly oval rooms with stone walls, stone benches and stone 'dressers'. The whole site has been very well preserved beneath a sand dune, right on the seashore. When the site was excavated in the 1930s it was thought to be an ordinary house where people lived, but Colin Richards (in the light of his own excavations at Barnhouse) has shown that it was a special house, and very carefully laid out. People may well have lived there, but they also worshipped their gods and the spirits of their departed ancestors.

The Stones of Stenness

There are two magnificent Neolithic stone circles on Orkney, the Ring of Brodgar and the Stones of Stenness. They were built at the same time as Stonehenge. Like Stonehenge there is a circular ditch and bank which surrounds the stones and marks out the special area where religious ceremonies took place. There is only one way through the Stenness ditch which is about 70 metres in diameter. Only four stones stand today at Stenness, but originally there were 12. Excavations in 1973–74 found a stone-built hearth at the centre of the stone circle and broken decorated Neolithic pottery identical to that found at Barnhouse nearby.

Maes Howe

Maes Howe is one of the finest, best preserved Neolithic tombs in Europe. The masonry of the stone walls is superb, and the blocks have been carefully shaped to fit together precisely. It has a fine stone-built roof and the main chamber is entered by a low stone-lined passage. Inside the chamber are tiny stone-built rooms known as cells where the bones of the dead were laid in peace.

Some of the enormous stones of the Stenness circle are still standing.

Skara Brae, the oldest 'village' in Britain was revealed in the 1920s, when a storm washed away the sand-hills that had covered it for 5000 years.

DISCOVERING ANCIENT SITES:
GEOPHYSICS

Nowadays there are a large number of hi-tech machines which can 'look' below the soil in sufficient detail to allow the archaeologist to decide where to dig. In the past, although they were not aware they were doing so, people upset the ground's natural state by almost everything they did. For example, when a fire was lit the heat changed the ground's ability to hold an electrical charge; or when a ditch was dug, the ground would later become better at conducting an electrical charge. Most of the 'geophysical' machines that archaeologists use today to detect these faint traces rely on measuring small electric currents very accurately. Recently scientists have also produced a type of radar which can 'look' below the ground with radio waves. It has already produced some very exciting results.

Filming at the Skara Brae houses. You can still see the cupboards, beds and storage sinks, all made from slabs of Orkney stone. Note the low doorway on the right.

An extraordinary place

Everybody has heard of Stonehenge, but Avebury is for most people an even more extraordinary place. It is far larger, its stones are more crude and massive, and the tall trees around it make the visitor feel tiny and unimportant. It is so large that a small village nestles within the surrounding ditch and bank. The whole thing (except the modern village of course) was built and used almost five thousand years ago, in the Neolithic period.

The main site at Avebury (in Wiltshire) consists of a huge, roughly circular ditch, with a high earth bank outside it. This type of site is found only in Britain and is known to archaeologists as a 'henge' (after Stone*henge*). The ditch and bank at Avebury were broken at four separate places (at 3, 6, 9 and 12 o'clock on a clock face) by gaps that were wide enough to take a road. Around the inside of the ditch are huge stones set on end in the ground, so that they stand upright, and within the area enclosed by the great outer ditch are two smaller circles of stones. These may have marked areas of special importance where religious ceremonies took place. These are just some of the things that can be seen at Avebury, but they are just the beginning— there is far more to see in the country outside the huge henge.

ARCHAEOLOGY AND THE LANDSCAPE

Archaeologists have realized for a long time that it is not always possible to understand what went on at a particular site if you look at that site on its own. It is rather like trying to understand life in modern London by just looking at Trafalgar Square. Future archaeologists would need to excavate Heathrow, railway stations, the M25 and suburban houses to have any idea of what life today is really like. The same goes for ancient places like Avebury: we will only understand what really happened there if we stand back and look at the landscape around it.

This view of Avebury in 2000 BC is based on the latest archaeological discoveries.

The Avebury landscape

Although it is the most spectacular place to visit, the great henge at Avebury is only one part of a very complicated landscape. Most landscapes today consist of fields, farms, roads, towns, villages, churches and other things. But in the distant past landscapes were often rather different. Sometimes

certain parts of the countryside were thought to be important to the gods or the spirits of the dead and in these areas people built dozens, or even hundreds, of religious places. These places could be circles of stones, or henges like Avebury, or great avenues of stones, and there are also impressive tombs and smaller graves. It is almost as if these landscapes were huge open air churches, except that people still ploughed their fields and grazed their animals around the various religious places.

Some of the religious places in the Avebury landscape were made from huge logs and cannot be seen from the ground, as after five thousand years they have now completely disappeared. But others can still be seen by visitors to the area.

Silbury Hill

Silbury Hill is the largest man-made mound in ancient Europe. It was constructed towards the end of the Neolithic period around 2500 BC and was built in three episodes, each time it was made higher than the last. The hill is well made and constructed with hidden chalk walls that prevent the sides from collapsing in heavy rain. It used to be thought that a burial would be found at the bottom of the centre of the hill and archaeologists dug tunnels to find it. But it was not there. There was no sign of a grave. In other words, the hill was not built to cover anything, but for its own sake – who knows why?

Sarsen stones

Many of the prehistoric religious places around Avebury make use of huge grey stones, known as sarsens. These stones originally lay on the surface and were removed, beginning in Neolithic times, to clear the land for fields and pasture. The largest stones were used for tombs and other holy places. The stones themselves were probably considered sacred.

The Sanctuary

The Sanctuary was a special religious place, but smaller than some of the others around it. It was placed on the top of a steep hill, called Overton Hill, close to the Ridgeway. It could have been a place where dead bodies were stored safely after being carried from their homes along the Ridgeway for

Silbury Hill, the largest prehistoric man-made mound in Europe. But what was it for?

burial, for feeding to the birds or for cremation at one of the larger religious places around Avebury. It originally consisted (around 3000 BC) of several rings of wooden posts which were later replaced (around 2300 BC) by sarsen stones. Today the stones have gone and are replaced by square blocks of concrete to show where they were. Some people think the structure was roofed. Late in its life the stone circle was joined to the great henge at Avebury by the stones of the West Kennet Avenue. This is a long and splendid ceremonial road, probably used to transport the dead towards the next world at Avebury.

Hauling a sarsen stone to its final destination with leather ropes and wooden rollers. These huge sarsen stones, called 'Grey Wethers', were dragged several kilometres to Avebury to create the great stone circle.

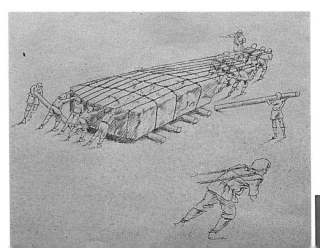

The mysterious Sanctuary lies at the end of the eastern avenue of Avebury. This is how it may have looked in 2000 BC.

The Ridgeway

The Ridgeway is the route of a very ancient road which ran along the crests of hills. It is known to have been important in Neolithic times, and may well be even older. The Ridgeway passes through the Avebury landscape and may be one of the reasons that the region became so important.

West Kennet long barrow

Today people are buried in churchyards or cemeteries, but in Neolithic times the dead were often buried beneath huge mounds, or barrows. Sometimes the mounds were round, but more often they were wedge-shaped and sometimes they contained rooms or chambers, in which bones or bodies were placed. The front of the tomb, known as the 'forecourt' was where the funeral ceremonies took place. At West Kennet the forecourt is backed by a wall of enormous sarsen stones that were used to block off the tomb after the last bodies had been placed in it, around 2200 BC.

Windmill Hill

Windmill Hill is probably the centre and the most sacred place of the special landscape. As early as 3300 BC the hilltop was marked-out from the rest of the landscape by three circular ditches, arranged one within the other. These ditches were not dug continuously, but in short lengths separated by a gap, or 'causeway'. From the air these strange ditches look rather like strings of sausages. In the ditches were found offerings or sacrifices of meat and food, together with human bones and skulls.

The West Kennet Avenue

Two of the four entranceways through the circular ditch and bank at Avebury were the routes of stone avenues. These were constructed quite late in the history of Avebury, around 2300 BC. Only one avenue survives today, and it runs from the south entrance to the great Avebury henge for over 2 kilometres up Overton Hill to the Sanctuary, where it ends. The stones marking the edges of the West Kennet Avenue are set about 15 metres apart, and some must have been considered sacred, as bodies have been found buried near them.

This Time Boy from prehistoric Avebury dances the deer dance to ensure good hunting, dressed in skins and wearing a necklace of bird and animal skulls. Some archaeologists study the customs of Native American peoples in the eighteenth and nineteenth centuries to provide an image of life in Western Europe in the late Stone Age, 5000 years ago.

HENGES

The word 'henge' was invented by archaeologists to describe a type of site that is only found in Britain and Ireland. Henges consist of a circular ditch with a bank on the outside. At one or two points (and rarely more) the ditch is broken by entranceways. Sometimes the area enclosed by the ditch and bank contains rings of stones or great wooden posts. Very often the outer ditch contains offerings of human bones or valuable objects. Henges were built in the Late Neolithic and Early Bronze Age periods, between about 2500 and 1600 BC.

When was the Bronze Age?

The Bronze Age in Britain started around 1800 BC, and followed the Neolithic or New Stone Age period; it continued until about 700 BC when the Iron Age began. These dates are very uncertain and the change from one Age to another was very gradual and probably extended over two or three generations. The Bronze Age is very important in British prehistory as it is the period when large areas of the countryside were cleared of forests and became fields and farms. Early in the Bronze Age people generally lived in very small groups, perhaps 2 or 3 families at the most, which were spread across the countryside from low-lying valleys to high up in the foothills of the mountains of Wales and Scotland. By the later Bronze Age these family groups had become larger, perhaps as many as 20 to 50 families in one place at a time. In many cases these small villages protected themselves from other villages or tribes with defences made from timber, rocks or earth.

What is bronze?

Bronze is an alloy, or a mixture of two or more types of metal. The main metal of bronze is copper, which is quite soft and when knives or axes are made of copper alone they soon become blunt. If about one part of tin is added to nine parts of copper, to make bronze, the metal is then very much harder and makes excellent axes, knives, swords, spearheads and even razors. When newly made, bronze objects are a wonderful glowing reddish-gold colour, but this gradually fades to a duller orange brown (unless it is kept carefully polished).

Flag Fen, 1000 BC. The Bronze Age inhabitants of Flag Fen constructed a massive wooden barrier to mark the boundary of their tribal territory. The great timbers have lasted for 3000 years in the waterlogged peaty soil. To the right are round dwelling houses built on dry land.

Using only a bronze axe which he made himself (seen leaning against the tree trunk), wooden wedges and a mallet, it took Francis Pryor 15 minutes to split this tree – just as the people of Flag Fen must have done it 3000 years ago.

Flag Fen

Flag Fen is on the eastern edge of Peterborough in an area now known as Eastern Industry. The site is just outside the modern city limits because the modern city buildings were built on more solid ground. The Bronze Age builders were able to build their constructions on soft watery land because they were made from light materials such as wood and thatch; such materials can also twist and bend as the soft ground below them moves. Modern buildings are made from steel or concrete and are very heavy and rigid.

In 1982 archaeologists found timbers in the side of a drainage ditch underneath the foundations of a Roman road in the middle of Flag Fen. After ten years' excavation we now know that these timbers formed part of a very large timber platform. A line of posts about 10 metres wide and 1 kilometre long ran right across Flag Fen and through the timber platform. The platform and the line of posts were constructed around 1350 BC and were maintained in use for 400 years, until 950 BC. The line of posts and the platform were first built as a huge fence to keep unwelcome people and their animals out of Flag Fen.

Later on the timbers of Flag Fen were the scene of religious ceremonies, where hundreds of valuable bronze objects were placed in the waters around them. Many of these objects had been deliberately broken before being offered to the waters. It is possible that some of the metal items were specially made at Flag Fen for this purpose. Human bones were found lying beside some of the posts; this discovery confirms that Flag Fen was an important religious site. Many of the animals bones found were from joints of beef, lamb or mutton. This meat was probably eaten during feasts.

Religion in the Bronze Age

After about 1500 BC, the middle years of the Bronze Age over most of Europe, including Britain, people began to place or throw valuable objects (usually of bronze) in watery places. This practice continued for over a thousand years, throughout the Iron Age and even into Roman times. One of the last legends of this ancient religious custom is the story of Sir Bedevere, one of King Arthur's knights of the Round Table, who hurled the sword Excalibur into deep water where it was caught by the Lady of the Lake.

Flag Fen in the Bronze Age

The waters of Flag Fen are next door to Fengate which is one of the most heavily settled parts of prehistoric Britain. At Fengate archaeologists have found many buried farms and fields that go back as far as 4000 BC. There were dozens of farms in the Bronze Age at Fengate and the waters of Flag Fen would have provided fish and wildfowl for food, particularly in the lean months of winter. Reeds and trees growing around the edges of the water were used for thatch and fuel. Hundreds, maybe even thousands of people would have visited Flag Fen regularly.

The farmers on the dry ground at Fengate, around the edge of Flag Fen, grew crops such as wheat and barley in fields now beneath the buildings of Peterborough. On the very edge of the waters they kept flocks of sheep and a few cows, pigs and horses. Their houses were round and roofed with reed and turf. There was a single doorway and a fire in the centre of the building, but no chimney or smoke-hole. Dry woods, especially willow, burn

RADIOCARBON DATING

Shortly after the Second World War an American scientist, Willard F. Libby, discovered that plants absorb small quantities of radioactive carbon dioxide gas (which is produced by the sun's rays in the earth's outer atmosphere) while they are growing. As soon as they die, the carbon they have absorbed from the gas begins to break down, like all radioactive substances. This process of radioactive decay happens at a known, constant, pace – which can be measured. It takes 5568 years for half the radioactive carbon to decay. So any ancient plant material (such as charcoal) that contains exactly half its original amount of radioactive carbon is 5568 years old; if it has less than half it is older, if it has more, it is younger. The bones of animals (which eat plants) can also be dated by radiocarbon.

with very little smoke. The walls were made from woven willow or hazel rods (known as wattle) which were smeared with a sticky mixture of clay, straw and cattle dung (known as daub).

The Fens

A fen is an area of wet ground where the water comes from a stream or river. A bog is also wet, but its water comes directly from rain; marshes are wet ground near the sea. Each type of wetland supports different plants and animals. Fens are famous for the richness and variety of their plants. Ancient pollen grains preserved in the peaty soils of Flag Fen show that there were as many as sixty types of flowering plants growing there in the Bronze Age. It would have been very beautiful with white and yellow waterlilies, guelder roses and, of course, flag irises (after which Flag Fen is named).

Some of the Bronze Age timbers have been gnawed-through by beaver (their very distinctive teeth-marks still survive clearly) and apart from frogs, newts and other animals common in the area today, Bronze Age people would have seen pelicans, sea eagles, sturgeons and otters.

The Fens were once Britain's largest wetland and cover about 400,000 hectares of land north and south of The Wash, mainly in south Lincolnshire

Some of the timbers of the platform at Flag Fen, as they were found by the archaeologists. Below are some of the finds from Flag Fen.

Clothing in the Bronze Age was made of rough, woven woollen material. Fragments have been found preserved in the moist ground. Music was provided with pipes made from the twigs of willow trees which grew abundantly locally.

and north Cambridgeshire. The Fens formed after the last Ice Age, around 7000 years ago as sea levels rose after huge areas of ice had melted in the warmer climate. Drainage of the Fens by humans started about 350 years ago and today they are almost entirely dry.

TREE-RING DATING

It is well known that you can tell the age of a tree by counting the rings that mark each year's growth. It is less well known that trees grow thicker rings in hot, wet summers and thin rings in cold, dry ones. Archaeological scientists have built up a history of these growth rings indicating wet and dry summers that covers most of Europe over the past 7000 years. This has been done by comparing the growth rings of living trees with those found in timber in old buildings and wells, and trees preserved in ancient bogs in very wet places. The best trees for tree-ring dating are oaks and the process of tree-ring dating is known as dendrochronology. Tree-ring dates are far more accurate than radiocarbon dates. At Flag Fen, for example, dendrochronology allows us to say that some trees were cut down in the *autumn* of the year 958 BC.

POLLEN ANALYSIS

On some summer days there is enough pollen in the air to make many people sneeze with hay fever. Most pollen grains are so tiny that they can only be seen under the microscope. But their outer skins are very tough indeed, and if an archaeological site is sufficiently damp these skins may survive for thousands of years. By counting the different types of pollen grains from an ancient site, archaeological botanists are able to construct an accurate picture of the types of plants that were growing in a particular region in the distant past. This process, known as 'pollen analysis' can be used to determine when forests were felled or when grass fields were ploughed-up.

Why are wet archaeological sites exciting?

Most archaeological sites consist only of things that will not rot, for example, stone, pottery, bricks, tiles and sometimes bones. But Flag Fen has remained wet until very recently and the wet peaty soil has protected the Bronze Age timbers from decay, by keeping them airless. In addition to three-thousand-year-old timbers, the wet soils of Flag Fen have preserved pollen grains, seeds, twigs and leaves. The microscopic plants, animals and fungi that normally cause wood to rot need air to breathe. Now that Flag Fen has been drained, this process has begun. The site is being excavated to record what was once there before it is too late. There will be very little left of Flag Fen in twenty years' time, unless something can be done to keep it wet.

What is there to see at Flag Fen today?

Flag Fen is open to the public throughout the year (including weekends and bank holidays) and visitors can see recreated Bronze Age buildings, fields and even live animals. A large lake has been made to keep about half of the buried timber platform wet and to preserve it for the future. There are displays of Bronze Age timbers and the visitor centre in the lake has a display of all the main finds made since 1982. These include a gold ring and bronze swords, daggers, spearheads, axes, brooches and other jewellery.

The Iron Age

Roman soldiers arrived in England in the year
AD 43. The people that confronted them were Celtic
tribesmen we know as the Ancient Britons. The
Celts were the native people of much of Europe and
they had a very rich and distinctive way of life. They
placed great importance on family ties and everyone
knew the details of their family's history. Families
were grouped together into tribes or clans and these
in turn were formed into small kingdoms. Some of
the names of these kingdoms were recorded by
Roman visitors: they are the first recorded names of
British history. Archaeologists have named this
Celtic period the Iron Age. The Iron Age starts
around 700 BC, with the arrival of the first iron
objects in Britain, and it ends, in England and
Wales, with the invasion of Roman troops in AD 43.
The Scots resisted the Romans more successfully, so
their Iron Age lasted much longer.

Celtic warriors

The Celts are commonly thought to have been a
people who enjoyed warfare and fighting. They
certainly built many defended hillforts, but
archaeologists have shown that evidence for actual
battles is rare. Many of the hillforts were probably
built to impress and frighten people, and were rarely
attacked. Most tribes and clans were too busy
farming the land and herding their sheep and cattle
to have much time for fighting. When fighting did
take place it was more like a dispute between two
families than all-out warfare. Neither family could
afford to lose its young men, so the dispute was
quickly settled. Weapons, such as swords and spears
were probably carried by older men to show their
importance.

Maiden Castle, Dorset, around AD 40. The great Iron Age hillfort provided a safe home for hundreds, perhaps
thousands of Ancient Britons. Maiden Castle was probably still the headquarters of a tribe called the Durotriges at the
time of the Roman invasion of Britain.

Every detail based on archaeological evidence, this is a scene of life on the summit of Maiden Castle around the time of Christ. A wooden palisade can be seen running along the ramparts in the background, providing added protection for the families and their dogs and chickens who live inside the hillfort.

Maiden Castle

Maiden Castle, in Dorset, is the most famous Iron Age hillfort in Britain. Iron Age hillforts were not like castles – they did not have high walls built of stone. They were built on the top of hills and were made of earth and rock which was dug out of the ground in deep and steep-sided ditches, which would have been very difficult to cross. The material dug from the ditches was then heaped up on the side of the ditch nearest the top of the hill. So if attackers managed to cross the ditch (and the defenders would be shooting arrows, throwing spears and slinging stones) they then had to climb the steep bank, known as a rampart. The ditches and banks were meant to keep enemies away from the top of the hill, as this was where the chief and his or her family were living, together with their relatives and other members of the clan.

The hill on which Maiden Castle was built dominates the landscape around it. This hill was an important place for people from about 3000 BC and it must have seemed the most sensible place to build Britain's largest hillfort. Maiden Castle was the main fort, or perhaps even the capital, of the Durotriges tribe. This was a powerful tribe who controlled much of what we now know as the county of Dorset.

When Maiden Castle was first built, at the beginning of the Iron Age, it was small and had just one ditch and bank. In the middle of the Iron Age the defenders doubled the fort's size and built three sets of massive ditches and ramparts. This enormous project took place about two centuries before the Roman invasion.

The fort's entrances

The weakest part of any fort or castle's defence is the entrance. That is why most castles that were built to be used by soldiers have only one way in or out. Maiden Castle has two entrances, one to the east and one to the west. They are very elaborate, with ditches and ramparts forming a complicated pattern, almost like a maze. Recent excavations by English Heritage have shown that the banks, or ramparts, around the entrances were fronted with wood, or, in places, stone walls. This must have been expensive and laborious work, but it must also have been very impressive indeed – especially to any visitor. The two entrances were not simply defensive; they were also meant to be spectacular and to frighten anyone, friend or foe, who might feel like causing trouble to the people who controlled the fort.

The cemetery

Maiden Castle was excavated by one of Britain's greatest archaeologists, Sir Mortimer Wheeler, in the summers of 1934 to 1937. In those days archaeologists did not have radiocarbon dating or many of the scientific tests available to modern archaeologists. Sir Mortimer discovered a cemetery of 52 graves at the eastern entrance to the fort, and quite reasonably thought that these were the graves of men who had died defending Maiden Castle against the attacking Roman soldiers. A very few of the men in the cemetery may well have died in battle against the Romans – one has a Roman spearhead in his back, and others have skulls with deep sword cuts. More than forty of the other bodies showed no signs of violent attack and were carefully placed in the ground with ornaments, jewellery and even food for the next world. Niall Sharples who recently excavated at Maiden Castle believes that the cemetery is not a 'war cemetery', as Sir Mortimer thought, but that it is the equivalent of a village or town cemetery that was in use for a long time before, and after, the Roman invasion. In other words, the Roman attack may not have been as bloody as we once thought.

Hurling sling-stones from the ramparts of Maiden Castle. The sling was one of the Ancient Britons' principal weapons.

The town within the fort

The hilltop inside the ditches and ramparts must have housed hundreds of people, who lived in round houses. At the beginning of the Iron Age the houses were spread across the ground, more or less at random, but later on they were built in neat rows. There were straight streets or roads, so that people could move about easily. Perhaps the most extraordinary thing about the town or village within the defences was the fact there were hundreds, perhaps even thousands, of deep pits – often deeper than a man's height – that had been dug into the chalk. These pits were used to store grain over winter, but in some cases human or animal bodies were thrown into them after they had gone out of use. This might suggest that the people considered that the pits (and what they contained) were very important, and that the gods who protected them had to be kept happy. The earth walls of the fort protected the tribe's grain supplies, as well as the people themselves.

Excavation has recovered the remains of ovens and hearths. There is lots of evidence that mutton and beef were eaten. The fields in which the crops were grown and where the animals grazed lay on the flatter land around the hillside. The inhabitants used fine pottery and decorated themselves with brooches made of bronze. There is evidence that blacksmiths were at work repairing and making iron tools for the farm, and probably weapons too. It seems to have been a very well-off community.

The latest excavations have shown that the small town that grew up inside the defences became very much smaller about fifty years before the Roman attack. In other words Maiden Castle may have become less important – and quite suddenly. So when the Romans attacked they may have thought that it was the capital town of the tribe, but they were probably wrong! It may have moved somewhere else by then.

Iron Age houses

Iron Age houses in Britain and Ireland were round with pointed, thatched roofs. A fire burned in the centre of the house which was large enough to hold

Making pottery. The Iron Age girl is inside a replica of an Iron Age round house, built by school-children at Cranborne, Dorset.

The Iron Age boy has blue patterns painted on his face and his hair is treated with lime to make it bushy and fierce. Modern archaeologists suggest that it was more important to prehistoric men and boys to *look* terrifying than to engage in all-out battle.

about a dozen people and the family pets. Farm animals, such as cattle, pigs, sheep and goats were usually housed in separate buildings. Round buildings are quite easy to build and are very strong; they also stand up well to storms and high winds. They have a high roof which can be used to hang hams, and other meats for smoking. Dry wood, which burns with far less smoke, can also be stored in the roofspace. Smoke from the fire found its way out through the roof and the doorway, but there was no chimney or smoke-hole. Floors were usually of beaten earth or clay. No actual Iron Age building survives, but archaeologists have built reconstructions which are warm, dry and snug – but sometimes a little smokey!

The Roman Empire

It has been said that the Romans brought civilization to barbarian Europe. They brought with them a uniform system of laws, a written language (Latin), written numbers, a ten-month calendar and fixed hours of the day. We are not sure how many of these things existed in Europe before the Romans, but we suspect that life was better-ordered than some Romans might have supposed. The important thing was that the Romans could *write* and the act of putting something down on paper, like putting something into a computer today, meant that people had to think more clearly. This type of clear thinking meant that people could organize how they were governed, or the way they should build a road, or set up new regiments in the army, and so on. The Romans were very well organized indeed. This did not make them very popular with everyone they met, or conquered.

The Romans introduced factory production of standardized goods made to a very high quality. For example, pottery, known as samian ware, which was a glossy pinkish-red in colour, was exported all over the Roman Empire, from factories in the south of France. Samian ware found today in France, Spain or Italy is exactly the same as that found in England. Along with factory production, the Romans built roads to distribute the goods they produced efficiently. They also introduced a system of money with which to pay for things. All the main elements of modern life were present in the Roman world.

DATES

Years before Christ are indicated by the letters BC (Before Christ) which are placed after the year's number. Years before Christ are numbered *backwards*; for example, the first visit of the Roman emperor Julius Caesar to Britain took place in 55 BC, his second visit was in 54 BC. After Christ, years are numbered forwards and are marked by the letters AD (Latin for *anno domini*, or 'year of Our Lord') which are placed before the year number, thus: AD 410 (the year the Romans actually left Britain).

Britain and Rome

England and Wales were a part of the Roman Empire for about 350 years, between AD 43 and AD 410. But it is a mistake to imagine that the entire population changed their way of life overnight, and began to talk Latin and wear Roman clothes. Some of the good things of Roman life, such as wine, reached the better-off people in Britain well before the invasion of AD 43. Archaeologists have found

ports on the south coast of England that specialized in importing fine continental food, drink, pottery and other items from the Roman world several decades before the actual Roman invasion. So Roman luxury goods were already fashionable in Britain.

When the Roman army invaded, life in the countryside remained the same: people continued to live in round houses and farmed the land much as they had always done. That is why archaeologists refer to the inhabitants of Roman Britain as 'Romano-British' – that is also the name given to the things they made and built. The period of time that the Roman army occupied Britain is referred to as the Roman *period*.

Roman soldiers building the granary at Birdoswald, a fort on Hadrian's Wall, Cumbria. You might see a scene like this on any building site today.

Hadrian's Wall — the edge of the Empire

After an initial period of turmoil and strife, which included the rebellion of the British Queen Boudica in the years AD 60–61, which nearly succeeded, Roman Britain settled down. Stable government, and good communication brought about by the newly-completed military roads, led to prosperity.

To people living outside, the Empire was a very desirable place. To the Romano-British authorities these people were a threat, but at the same time, both sides wished to trade. So the Romans established a wall close to the modern border between England and Scotland. This wall had at least three purposes. Firstly it reminded everyone, both in the Roman Empire and outside it, that the Roman Empire, with its army, was an extremely powerful and impressive force. Secondly, it formed an actual stone barrier to keep unwanted intruders outside the Roman province of Britain. Thirdly, it controlled access into the Empire: visitors left their swords there when they entered the province. They also paid any customs duty or taxes that the authorities required.

Hadrian's Wall was built in the second century AD to define the northern frontier of the Roman Empire in Britain. Long stretches of the Wall still stand to a height of 2 metres.

The Emperor's Wall

Hadrian's Wall was built on the personal instructions of the Emperor Hadrian immediately upon his return to Rome from a tour of the western Empire that had included a visit to the province of Britain. This visit took place in AD 122, and work on the wall started very shortly afterwards. The Emperor, who came to power in AD 117, was a soldier himself, and he was keen to improve the army's morale and to make it even more professional. At the same time that he ordered the construction of Hadrian's Wall he also ordered the reinforcement and enlargement of border defences in Germany. The wall was not constructed and finished in one operation and, like many great works of military engineering, it eventually proved to be far more expensive both to build and to man, than had been originally estimated. When finally completed it is thought that as many as 5000 soldiers were required to guard, supply and look after the wall. These men had to be paid with money raised from taxes.

The Wall — some vital statistics

Hadrian's Wall was one of the wonders of ancient Britain, and much of it survives to be seen today. It ran from the North Sea to the Irish Sea for 117 kilometres (73 miles). It was about 3 metres thick and 5 metres high. At first, the eastern part of the wall was built of stone and the western part from turf, but later the turf lengths were replaced with stone. The wall had to cross two large rivers on arched stone bridges. From these bridges the defenders on the wall could easily have controlled all traffic along and across the rivers.

The Wall's defences

The wall itself was sufficiently high to provide a good barrier, but it could be crossed quite easily by a larger group and it was decided from the beginning to fortify the wall in a way that would house and shelter the troops who manned the defences. The precise layout of the wall's defences varied from place to place, but when it was originally planned there were to be three elements: a ditch, turrets and milecastles.

The ditch was steep-sided and was dug on the northern side of the wall. This was the direction from which trouble could be expected. At every Roman mile (slightly shorter than a modern mile) a milecastle was built. These miniature forts were on the south side of the wall and each one had a tower that defended a gateway through it. A few troops were housed in the milecastles whose main purpose was to control access through the gateway. Between each milecastle were two defended towers or turrets. The effect of the turrets and milecastles was to provide a strong, defended point every ⅓ of a mile along the wall.

The forts

A series of 17 forts was added to the wall along its entire length at regular, but not precise, distances. We know from stones with carved inscriptions found in the walls of the forts that construction had certainly started by the year AD 126. The forts were, in effect, small fortified military towns. They were shaped rather like a playing card, with rounded corners and an entranceway on each side. The outer wall was made of stone or turf and there was usually a steep-sided ditch on the outside, just like Hadrian's Wall itself. Buildings within the fort included the Commanding Officer's headquarters, barracks (dormitories) for the soldiers, workshops,

a hospital and a large granary. This granary held enough grain to keep the soldiers supplied for a year – probably several hundred tons. The fort at Birdoswald, for example, had a garrison of 1000 people.

A drawing of a portrait of the Emperor Hadrian. This is all that remains of a life-size statue of the emperor. It was dredged from the river Thames.

Replica of a miniature horseman and rider – a Roman child's toy?

THE ROMAN ARMY

The Roman army was successful because it was well organized, well armed and (most important of all) well disciplined. The main unit of men was the legion which consisted of 5300 soldiers; each legion consisted of ten cohorts and each cohort held six centuries (commanded by a centurion) of 100 men each (when you add them up the sums do not work out, because the first cohort was composed of double-sized centuries). The ordinary soldiers, or legionaries, were often recruited from conquered peoples, but the Roman military authorities liked to transfer these legions away from their native countries – to somewhere else where they would be less likely to rebel and cause trouble. Soldiers were expected to fight, but they also had to build their own forts, roads and defences. Hadrian's Wall was built and manned by Roman soldiers.

The Saxons

The Saxons (or Anglo-Saxons, to use their full name) began to arrive in Britain in the later years of the Roman period. Roman rule officially ended in the year AD 410, but it had begun to break up long before then. The Anglo-Saxons were northern Europeans who mainly came directly across the North Sea, from places in and around modern Holland. Some were invited to Britain as paid soldiers (or mercenaries) by the authorities who were worried about maintaining law and order as the Roman system of government began to break down. Others simply sailed across the sea.

The years after the collapse of the Roman Empire in western Europe are sometimes known as the Dark Ages, because written history can throw very little light upon them. Not many people were writing things down, and life in many ways went back to what it had been like in the Iron Age, immediately before the Roman invasion. There is no evidence that life in the Dark Ages was particularly cruel or brutal. It was just different from life in Roman times.

The Early Saxon Period

The Saxon period in England lasts from the collapse of Roman rule until the Norman Conquest of 1066. The 600 years of the Saxon period are divided into three sub-periods, each of about 200 years, called the Early, Middle and Late Saxon periods. The Early Saxon period is the least understood, as there are very few ancient written accounts of it, so archaeology is very important. In England, most of the Romano-British population had become Christian, but in the Early Saxon period there was a return to pre-Christian beliefs. That is why the period used to be known as the Pagan Saxon period. Saxon society was very different from Romano-British society, and had more in common with the Iron Age, which had continued throughout the Roman period in those parts of northern Europe that were not taken into the Roman Empire. Although the Saxons had their roots in pre-Roman times, their lifestyle was not at all primitive.

West Heslerton: a huge excavation

Dominic Powlesland and his team have been excavating at West Heslerton, in Yorkshire, for about 15 years. During that time they have uncovered millions of finds and have caused archaeologists to rethink many of their ideas on how the Early and Middle Saxons lived. The team at West Heslerton use huge earthmoving machines to remove the modern soil, an inch at a time. Every bucketful of earth removed by the machines is watched by archaeologists and as soon as there is any sign of ancient remains, the machine is stopped, and careful excavation begins.

The excavations have produced some very fine objects, including decorated bone combs, bronze brooches and large quantities of broken pottery. The richest finds come from non-Christian graves. These grave-goods, such as brooches and meat bones, were meant to accompany the dead person into the next life, so some objects were very beautifully made.

The archaeologists and students work very carefully. They record where everything was found and enter the information directly into hand-held computers, on the spot. The computers also help to produce drawings and plans of what was found. Lasers are used in the map-making, as well. All this modern technology is required to make sense of the hundreds of thousands of finds that are discovered each year.

The Saxon village at West Heslerton around AD 600, based on archaeological discoveries. The industry is located in the foreground, with the houses beyond, across the stream.

West Heslerton – the biggest 'dig' in Europe.

English villages

Most modern English villages can be traced back to Saxon times. Sometimes it is simple to show when a village was first inhabited – its name can give it away. Names that end in *ton*, such as Weston (there are 16 Westons in England), are derived from the Anglo-Saxon word *tun*, meaning a farm or village. So Weston originally meant 'the west village'. West Heslerton originally meant 'the west village where hazel bushes grow'. In the east of England the Vikings established many villages in the Saxon period and their Norse word for *tun* was *by* – this is why there are so many places in Lincolnshire with names such as Grimsby.

Saxon villages

Saxon villages played a very important part in the development of the English landscape. It used to be thought that they were all new places, without any earlier history, but archaeologists have shown that almost every village that has been examined has produced evidence for Roman or pre-Roman occupation. These earlier settlements were often less permanent than the Saxon villages, which is why they have escaped attention. Most of their original Celtic or Romano-British names have been replaced by the familiar Saxon ones.

West Heslerton is unusual because it shows clear evidence for planning: certain areas were set aside for particular types of buildings and industrial or farming activities. It is as if a person, or group of people, had the power to decide what was to take place – and where. This was a very unexpected discovery by the archaeologists.

Buildings

The best-known type of Saxon building has a large rectangular pit or hole dug beneath the floor. They are often called sunken featured buildings, or SFBs for short. When they were first excavated, in Germany, it was thought that they were 'pit dwellings' and that the people actually lived in the hole, with a roof over them. It was then realized that the hole would soon get damp and unpleasant, and no remains of steps or stairs were found. We now understand that the purpose of the pit was to allow air to pass freely around the wooden floor, as a way of stopping wet-rot. If the floorboards had been placed directly on the ground they would have rotted in a few years.

These houses with pits under the floor are only found in the Early Saxon period. More conventional wooden buildings are found throughout Saxon times, and these were made in a variety of sizes, but all were rectangular. Some 150 buildings have been found at West Heslerton. They had thatched roofs and looked rather like some of the older barns you can still see on farms today. Archaeologists can plan the layout of these buildings by finding the holes that were dug to hold their wall posts (the posts themselves have long-since vanished). The ground plans of many hundreds of Saxon houses are now known and they are all similar and are built in sizes, and multiples of sizes, that occur again and again. It is almost as if Saxon builders used pattern books, or kits. More probably, carpenters were well-trained during their apprenticeship and learned the correct way of erecting a timber building that would last for a long time.

Saxons were buried with their precious possessions, for use in the after-life (left). On the right, Now Boy, Graham Horner, lies in a mock grave with his personal stereo, his favourite mug and his Blue Peter badge!

Saxon cloth

The Saxons wove fine woollen cloth. At West Heslerton there is evidence for weaving provided by dozens of clay and stone weights. Each weight has a hole through it. These weights hung below a loom and were used to keep the fabric being woven taut. We know about Saxon fabrics from a few waterlogged pieces found in towns such as York, and from early written accounts. But most of the fabrics from Early Saxon times have survived in a strange way as 'corrosion products'.

PRESERVATION IN 'CORROSION PRODUCTS'

Cloth that has been in contact with damp metal for a long time is preserved in the metal's 'corrosion products'. The best known 'corrosion product' is rust, but bronze also produces a bright greenish-blue type of rust, which is very poisonous. In the damp soil of a grave, for example, a dead man's cloak will gradually turn green where it touches his shield or sword. After a long time the green colour spreads as the 'rust' continues to be produced by the corrosion of the metal. Soon the cloak itself rots away, and all that remains are the fossilised scraps that were touching metal. So when archaeologists find metal objects in a grave they are careful to look for traces of well-preserved fabric in any 'rust'.

The sons of Norman nobles would be expected to be proficient with the long, or 'Danish', bow.

On the morning of 14 October 1066, the invading forces of William of Normandy ('the Conqueror') attacked Harold's Saxon army on a hillside north of Hastings. Eight hours later, the course of European history had changed for ever.

A famous date in English history

The battle of Hastings took place on 14 October 1066. All the kings and queens of England can trace their ancestry from King William the Conqueror. To many people, 1066 is a very early date in English history; to some it is even the beginning. But to archaeologists it is a very late date in the story of England. By 1066 there had been towns in England for over a thousand years; there had been farms and small villages for at least four thousand years. There were also roads, laws, central government and possibly castles in pre-Norman, or Saxon, England.

The Norman Conquest brought to England a strong king with a very powerful group of loyal supporters. The new system worked well when the king was strong and fair, but some of William I's successors were weak – and the result was nearly chaos.

What if the Normans had lost the Battle of Hastings?

By the year 1066 there were large numbers of Viking settlers living in England. The Saxons who came before them were also from northern Europe. If King Harold had won the battle, England would most probably have become a part of Scandinavia and the Viking world. It was the Norman Conquest that drew England into the mainstream of European history.

The Saxon Kings of England

Before the *Roman* conquest of AD 43 a very large part of southern England was united under a powerful king, Cunobelin, into one kingdom. The Romans completed the task and England became a single province of the Roman Empire for 350 years. After the collapse of the Roman Empire, England again split up into a series of perhaps seven smaller kingdoms, as in pre-Roman times. After about 200 years the seven kingdoms were reduced to three main kingdoms: Wessex, Mercia and Northumbria. King Offa of Mercia was one of the greatest Saxon Kings, but after his death in 796 Viking raids and invasions removed eastern England from Saxon control. So England and Wessex became one and the same thing.

The greatest of the Wessex Saxon kings was King Alfred the Great and he, with his three sons who followed him, established England as a kingdom. More Viking raids followed, and the throne of England was even occupied by Viking kings – King Cnut (1017–35) was the most important of these. After the long, rather weak reign of King Edward the Confessor (1042–66), the throne was taken by King Harold who only ruled for 10 months. During that short time King Harold established a reputation as a vigorous and successful monarch. The Battle of Hastings ended his reign.

Why the battle happened

When kings and queens died there was often a problem of who was to take over. The only way to avoid this problem is to have rules of succession which clearly lay down who should inherit the throne. King Edward the Confessor died after a long reign without any children – so it was difficult to decide who should follow him on the throne. The two best claims were from foreign relatives, one from Norway, and the other, successful in the end, from France.

William the Conqueror (or Duke William as he was known earlier) was a close friend and relation of the Saxon King Edward the Confessor who died in January 1066. Edward is known to have wanted Duke William to be the next king, but at the last minute he was advised to change his mind and named Earl Harold of Wessex instead. Harold was commander of the English army and a very good soldier, but he had no royal blood.

The battle

On Monday, 25 September King Harold defeated the troops of the Norwegian contender to his throne, King Harold Hardrada of Norway, at the battle of Stamford Bridge, in Yorkshire. He then turned his victorious soldiers south and after a rapid and exhausting march his tired men arrived at the site of the Battle of Hastings to face the fresh Norman troops on Friday, 13 October. Both armies numbered some six to seven thousand troops. The English army fought on foot, whereas the Normans had two or three thousand soldiers on horseback. Battle began at nine o'clock on Saturday morning 14 October.

Harold's troops were drawn up in a line close to where the abbey buildings were later built; Duke William's forces were on the other side of a small stream along the valley side (parallel to the modern road). The battle raged all day, the Normans bravely attacking, and the English stubbornly defending. Duke William's brother, Bishop Odo, was a religious man and it was not considered right that he should carry a sword. So he wielded a huge wooden club which he swung around with both hands in a most fearsome manner. Eventually Harold's two brothers were killed and in the early evening the King himself was cut down. The English resistance then collapsed. King William I was crowned the next day, like all later English kings and queens, in London, at Westminster Abbey.

Battle Abbey

About four years after the battle, King William I decided to found a monastery on the site of his great victory. This would be in memory of the dead, but it would also attract people to the area and help to defend a stretch of countryside from any other possible invaders. Four monks from the Benedictine abbey of Marmoutier in France were the first members of what would soon become a thriving monastic community. Work on the abbey was funded by the King and a small part of the abbey church was consecrated ten years after the battle itself.

The completed abbey church was consecrated in February 1094, in the presence of the Conqueror's son, William II. The Conqueror left Battle Abbey a fortune on his death and also granted it all the land within a radius of one-and-half miles of the high altar in the abbey church. This gift ensured that the abbey remained prosperous for its entire life, until 1538, when Henry VIII closed all the monasteries.

A few years after the Battle of Hastings, King William built an abbey on the site of his victory, at a place that came to be called Battle.

The Bayeux Tapestry, made after 1066 to commemorate William's victory over the English, follows every stage of the invasion and the battle in wonderful detail. It is one of our main sources of information about the Battle of Hastings.

The Benedictine Order

The monks of Battle Abbey belonged to the Benedictine Order and lived out their lives following the rules laid down by St Benedict just over 500 years earlier. These rules gave order and peace to the monks' lives in times that were often harsh and troubled. Each day was lived following an 'horarium' or daily timetable. This would vary according to the season of the year, but included time for scholarly work, for reading and, of course, for prayer, which took place several times a day in the abbey church. Unlike some later monastic orders, the Benedictines did not place great emphasis on physical work in the fields or gardens. So they needed practical support from the town, which supplied the monastery with food, clothing and fuel.

The town of Battle

The small town of Battle was set up to look after the monastic community of Battle Abbey. Its High Street lines up on the main monastery gateway and its shops and craftsmen supplied the needs of the monastic community. Many of the sons of Battle families became monks and the two communities relied closely upon one another.

Orphan boys were sometimes 'given' to an abbey to be brought up by the abbot. Known as oblates, they were taught to read and write and might become monks in later life. Here a quill pen is sharpened with a pen-knife.

The medieval village of Cosmeston, near Penarth in South Wales, was reconstructed on the very foundations of the original village, uncovered by archaeologists. Only authentic materials were used in the rebuilding.

The Black Death

Many of the deserted medieval villages of England and Wales were abandoned 600 to 700 years ago, after a long period when the population had grown steadily. Many villages were established on poor land and a series of bad harvests in the early fourteenth century led to widespread famine. Under these conditions health is poor and disease spreads rapidly. The Black Death (bubonic plague) arrived in 1348 and soon spread across the land. It continued to attack for another 150 or so years. By the end of the epidemic the population had fallen by a half, and many villages were abandoned.

Cosmeston — a typical deserted medieval village

The little village of Cosmeston lies just outside Penarth on the south Wales coast. Today traffic rushes past the village on a straight modern road. The original road wound its way through the centre of the village. Almost nothing remained of the village after its abandonment, and its reconstruction is entirely based on the discoveries of archaeologists who have excavated the foundations of some of the

Now Girl Liz Thomas gets a lesson in bread-making from Time Girl Sarah McCann.

Southampton in the thirteenth century. English Street, home of the le Flemyng family, runs down to the busy harbour. The merchants' vaults lay beneath these fine town houses. (**See pages 38–9.**)

buildings. They have since rebuilt many of the buildings, sometimes using their original foundations.

The medieval countryside

At Cosmeston the fields of the countryside were laid out in a very carefully-organized manner. Each house or homestead sat in its own block of land, called a croft. These were about half a hectare in size. Around the village were the huge common fields where the peasants also owned or farmed land. This land was managed on a rotation system — crops such as wheat were followed by barley and beans. Every fourth year the field was rested, and used for grazing. Some of the land around the village belonged to the lord of the manor and peasants were

not allowed to graze their animals, or hunt there. Part of this land was woodland that was carefully managed and looked after to provide timber for buildings, and wood for fuel.

Life in the country

Everyone in the village at Cosmeston would have worked together at harvest-time and the crops were stored in barns belonging to the villagers, the priest and the lord. The grain was milled to make bread which was baked in the kilnhouse. The houses were built from local materials: the walls were made from stone gathered at Lavernock beach nearby, and the roofs were thatched with local reed. These buildings were warm and dry, but not very bright, especially in winter.

Dovecot

A large stone-built dovecot stood on a hill overlooking the village. This was one of the finest buildings in the village and housed hundreds of doves, that belonged to the lord of the manor. The doves were kept for their eggs, for their droppings which made excellent fertilizer, and for their meat— particularly in the lean months of winter.

Life in the town

In the countryside of medieval England many of the ordinary people were tied to the lord of the manor of their village by laws that prevented them from leaving, and told them where and when they could work. By modern standards they were not at all free. Things were different in the towns and cities, where people had very much more freedom to do as they pleased. Medieval towns relied on

The medieval dovecot belonging to the lord of the manor at Cosmeston would have housed hundreds of birds, kept for food and feathers. The building was more substantial than many of the villagers' homes. (**See pages 36–7.**)

trade for their prosperity. The villages around them traded grain, wool, timber and other items for things that could not be produced locally, such as fine cloth, wine, silverware, costly furniture and so on. That is why most towns were on main roads or rivers. Some, such as Southampton, were sea ports.

Guilds

The men who organized the trade, who found both the customers for and the producers of exotic goods, were the merchants. In good years merchants could make a lot of money from their trade, but in bad years life became very difficult indeed. That is why most merchants belonged to a Guild. These organizations helped merchants become established in their trade, they kept unwelcome outsiders from joining it, and also helped in hard times. In modern terms the guilds provided merchants with banking, insurance and social security, all in one. There were guilds for all sorts of people, and not just the rich and powerful. In Southampton, for example, the porters who unloaded the ships and moved the goods to the warehouses belonged to their own guild – which acted very much like a modern trades union.

The Southampton merchants

Dr Andy Russel has been excavating a medieval merchant's house in the old High Street. Nothing survives of the original building above ground, but below ground four large vaults have survived from medieval times, almost intact. This is due to the great strength of their arched roofs. The building is known to have belonged to a rich merchant called le Flemyng who traded in a variety of things, such as wine, gemstones, wool and fabrics.

In medieval times the dockside was just a minute's walk from the le Flemyng house and storage vaults, but today the town has spread into the old dock areas and the sea has been driven back a long way. The old sea frontage would have been at the end of a street aptly named Porters Lane, as this was where the porters rolled barrels of wine from the ships back to the High Street.

From old documents we know the names of Walter le Flemyng's real children — Alice and John. The steps in the background once led to Walter's private chamber.

DISCOVERY FROM THE AIR

A large number of medieval villages can be found on early maps, but cannot be seen on the ground. They have been deserted, and the buildings have disappeared above ground level, but archaeologists have found ways of rediscovering them. Sometimes the faint outlines of collapsed barns and cottages can be spotted from the air as low humps and bumps. Sometimes ploughing has removed even these slight traces. Ploughed, and completely flat, deserted villages can be spotted from the air by the distinctive way that crops such as wheat and barley grow. At ground level stinging nettles show where manure was heaped up and where people grew their vegetables. Dark patches show where old farmyards once stood, and roads show as pale lines in the crop. These patterns in growing crops are known as cropmarks. They are best seen from an aeroplane in May and June, but they can also be seen from upstairs in a house or double-decker bus. Cropmarks show up best in dry years. Some archaeologists are expert at spotting ancient sites from the air and fly around the country in small planes, taking thousands of photographs of their latest discoveries.

The discovery of Walter le Flemyng's private loo! Medieval cess-pits contain all sorts of objects which interest archaeologists.

The great formal gardens of Kirby Hall in Northamptonshire were laid out for Sir Christopher Hatton in the late seventeenth century. Their ground plan was rediscovered by archaeologists in the 1980s and the gardens are now being restored. Much of the magnificent mansion is in ruins today but is cared for by English Heritage.

A very grand house

Kirby Hall is a very grand house indeed. If it had been built by a royal Duke or Prince it would have been called a palace. Today the house is a deserted ruin, looked after by English Heritage, but four hundred years ago it was bustling with life and excitement. The house itself is built out of limestone that was quarried nearby; some was even dug out of the garden! The local limestone is a very good building material and the fine carvings that decorate the outside of Kirby Hall are almost as fresh as they would have appeared in the days of Queen Elizabeth I.

Houses are not just places where people live. In the past, just as today, people's houses told the world how important they, and their family, were (or think they were). We are meant to believe that important people live in large, splendid houses. In the time of Queen Elizabeth I many people were

making money in new ways: as merchants, by trading, by shipping and so forth. Some of these people had no Royal family connections and were keen to show Queen Elizabeth, and King James I (who followed her), just how important and loyal they were. So they built enormous and very highly decorated buildings, like Kirby Hall. Many were so huge and expensive to maintain that they eventually collapsed. This is what happened at Kirby Hall.

Sir Humphrey Stafford

The building of Kirby Hall was started by Sir Humphrey Stafford in 1570. Sir Humphrey's grand building was not completed when he died just five years later in 1575. His family were horrified at the cost and sold the still unfinished building to its most famous owner, Sir Christopher Hatton I, for £4000 – a huge sum of money in those days.

The Dancing Chancellor

Sir Christopher Hatton I bought Kirby Hall when he was just 35. Shortly after he purchased Kirby, he started to build another huge house at Holdenby, just a few miles away. He built Holdenby largely to entertain Queen Elizabeth I in lavish splendour. He only visited Holdenby about every two years, and went to Kirby even less often. He was a great favourite of the Queen and eventually became her Lord Chancellor (or Prime Minister). It was said that he had 'the shapliest legs in England' and he was reputed to be an excellent dancer. The Queen certainly enjoyed his company, but when he died, in 1591, he owed her huge sums of money — most of which had been spent building houses for her entertainment!

After the death of the first Sir Christopher, the house passed to other members of the family (mostly called Christopher) who continued to enlarge it. King James I stayed there three times as a guest of Sir Christopher Hatton II, and was entertained with royal splendour. The King also visited Kirby as the guest of Sir Christopher III in 1620.

In the seventeenth century the formal gardens would have required a large staff to maintain them. The head gardener's boy carries his leather tool bag and his young mistress's pet canary.

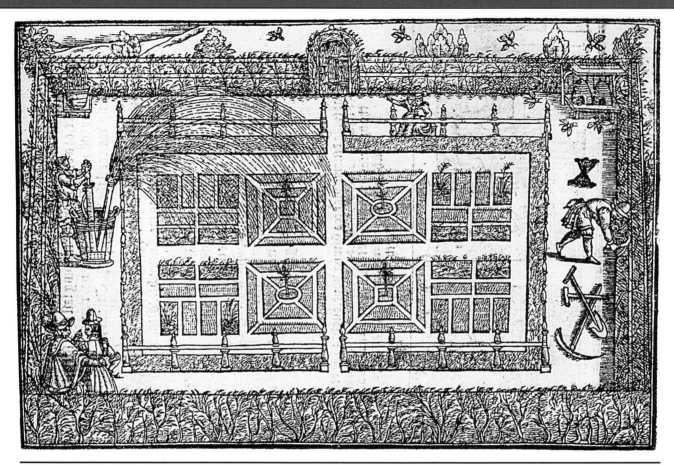

English landowners borrowed the idea of the formal garden with cut-out patterns from great gardens in other countries of Europe.

The Great House — a small town

Great houses in the 1500s and 1600s were largely self-sufficient. Huge gardens supplied vegetables, water came from wells, wheat and barley were grown by local farms and nearby villages provided staff and servants. The staff lived in the house and around it and most of the people living near a great house depended on it for their livelihood. Just as today, many houses were open to passing travellers, who could look around and be impressed by the importance and good taste of the people who lived there. As everyone depended on the house and its owner, few people raised objections when things were done that nobody would tolerate today.

The fine clothes worn by the ladies and gentlemen would be harmed by walking in the rain, so during the winter walks were taken along the Long Gallery on the first floor. The windows of this room looked out across the great formal garden.

GARDENS

Today archaeologists are restoring the gardens to their former glory. An excavation was carried out by Brian Dix and his team who were able to trace the layout of long-vanished paths by following the pattern of nails that were used to fix edging-boards into position around the lawns. In the early 1600s gardens were often designed from pattern-books, just as today we would choose wallpaper. These gardens were intended to look attractive from the ground and from the windows of the Long Gallery.

The gardens, like the house, were elaborate and were constructed to impress visitors. Sometimes their construction involved the removal of buildings that were thought to be unsightly. At Kirby Hall we know that a church and its graveyard were demolished to make way for the gardens. Several houses were also removed.

Waterworks

Many of the formal gardens of the period included elaborate water features, such as lakes, ponds, canals and fountains. At Kirby Hall, the brook which runs through the garden was dammed and an elaborate sluice-gate was constructed so that the water level could be kept high. This made the little brook appear like a wide, flat river. A fine garden house, or pavilion, was constructed so that visitors could sit and admire the water and the gardens beyond.

Children

Upper class children in the sixteenth and seventeenth centuries dressed like miniature adults. Girls were strapped into tight corsets beneath beautiful dresses, and boys wore silk stockings and fine polished shoes. These were not clothes suitable for playing in. The children of the farm workers and house servants went barefoot and were ragged, and probably cold in winter, but at least they could move about freely.

From her window young Elizabeth Hatton, the daughter of Sir Christopher, would have gazed out upon a 'classical' garden landscape. She is recreated here by local schoolgirl Charlotte Hubback. The entire village of Kirby, its church and its graveyard were demolished to make room for the pleasure of the Hatton family.

British industry in Victorian times

Britain in Victorian times was the richest and most powerful country in the world. The Industrial Revolution had started in England, in the eighteenth century, and towards the end of the nineteenth century British industry was using vast quantities of raw materials. Some of these raw materials came from abroad, from countries in the Empire, but many came from the British Isles. The best-known locally produced industrial materials were coal and iron, but other materials were also in constant demand. Of these, the heavy metal lead was one of the most important.

Lead mining in the North Pennine Hills

Lead has never been easy to mine. It comes from a mineral called galena which is quite commonly found below the ground in the North Pennine Hills of England. Lead mining may have started in the region in Roman times, but there is still no good evidence for this. We do know that lead mining was already important in medieval times, by the early thirteenth century. The early miners extracted most of the ores that could easily be mined from the surface. By the later years of Queen Victoria's reign the shallower deposits had been mined out, and only the deeply buried ores remained.

The Park Level Mine at Killhope is a good example of one of the larger deep mines in the region. Today it stands on its own, near the head of the river valley, but in Victorian times it would have been just one of many. Apart from Killhope, which has been extensively restored since 1980, many of the old mine buildings have been destroyed, to provide materials for other buildings, or else have been reused as barns and cowsheds for the many farms that now occupy the landscape. Today the spectacular country around Killhope is green, pleasant and peaceful. A hundred years ago the sky would have been filled with smoke and the sounds of crashing and hammering. Heavily-laden carts rumbled along the rough roadways. Hundreds of men and boys hurried about their daily work, above and below the ground.

Boys of nine and ten worked, almost like slaves, on the washing floor at Killhope lead mine, County Durham, 120 years ago. They separated the lead ore — the galena — from the stone which came from the mine. Old military uniforms, discarded after the Crimean War, sometimes provided work clothes for the men and boys.

It was not unusual for girls and women to walk 10 miles over the fells to and from their small-holdings, bringing fresh food to their fathers and brothers working in the mine.

Work below the ground

Coal mines and lead mines are very different. Coal is found in horizontal layers known as *seams*. These seams are usually mined in tunnels, often known as galleries, which are reached by a deep shaft. Lead ore is found in vertical *veins*, which may be followed down from the surface in deep shafts or pits. Some veins run deep into the hills and these may be reached by tunnels driven into the hillside. When the tunnellers reach the vein they can then follow it upwards or downwards. Like coal mining, lead mining is a very dangerous process.

The main danger to people working deep underground is from water and the miners took elaborate precautions against flooding. Sometimes they built underground water-wheels to power pumps that kept the mineshafts dry. But in dry weather the water-supply to the wheels dried up, so the pumps stopped – and the mines deep below flooded. Horses and ponies were often used to pull carts of ore out of the mine. At Killhope the carts were eventually replaced by a horse-drawn narrow-gauge railway.

One of the most dangerous jobs was actually extracting the ore from the vein, by hand. If the ore was soft enough it could be removed with a pick-axe. This was hard work. More often the ore and rock was so hard that it had to be blasted out, with explosives (gunpowder). In order to do this a hole had to be drilled with an iron bar or *jumper* that was repeatedly hit with a heavy hammer. This work was done by teams of two men – one held the jumper, while the other hit it with a hammer. The hole was then packed with gunpowder and fired. Fuses were unreliable and often the blast went off early. Many men lost hands, arms and eyes in this way. The mine was completely dark and all of this work took place by the light of just two or three candles. It was not surprising that lead miners rarely lived to be more than fifty years old.

WHAT LEAD WAS USED FOR

Lead is a heavy metal that corrodes (or rusts) very slowly indeed. It also melts at a low temperature. In the past these properties made it a very suitable material for making water pipes that would never rust or leak. They could be mended on the spot with heat provided by a simple wood fire. Unfortunately nowadays we know that lead is also poisonous and that unpurified water from lead pipes can cause lead poisoning. Plumbers, who work with pipes and drains, get their name from *plumbum*, the Latin word for lead. Sheet lead is still used for sealing roofs, but it is very expensive. Lead is also used for making rifle bullets, where its weight helps each shot to go in a straight line. In Victorian times Britain had huge armed forces and lead would have been in constant demand.

Killhope lead-mining centre today. Visitors come here to see the lead workings and try their hand at labouring on the washing floor.

Work above the ground

Removing the ore from under the ground was just the start of the process. This work was done by men. Most of the work that took place on the surface was done by boys. The surface work usually took place near the mouth of the mine and involved the removal of waste rock so that clean galena could be sent to the smelters for conversion into lead. Lead ore is not itself poisonous, but the smelting process (that converts ore to metal) was extremely dangerous and produced deadly fumes. Smelters were therefore placed on high hills, had tall chimneys and were positioned well downwind of towns and villages.

Surface work took place on the washing floor. Ore or 'bouse' from the mine was crushed by boys, using flat hammers. It was a very boring job that was supervised by the eagle-eye of the master-washerman. Nobody fooled around when he was there. The crushed bouse was then washed in water and the heavy lead-bearing galena fell to the bottom, and could be separated out. This is the same principle that prospectors use when 'panning' for gold.

The Great Wheel

By 1876 the output of the mine and washing floors had increased so much that a new crushing mill was built to speed-up the process. A huge water-wheel was built to power the crushing mill machinery and it was powered by an elaborate network of water courses dug by hand. Today the Killhope wheel is the only surviving example of a type that was common a hundred years ago. Some were even bigger!

Miner-farmers

Some of the miners were also small farmers, who lived locally. They and their sons would stay at the mine for several days at a stretch and food would be brought to them from the farmhouse. These people were usually very poor and the food was barely nourishing. But they were still expected to work in the mine for twelve or more hours a day.

Life at the mine

The men and boys who worked at the mine often lived in a communal bedroom known as the lodging shop. Men and boys slept five to a bed and cooked in this room. Their dirty clothes were dried in front of the fire and gave off clouds of harmful dust. Every night the chorus of coughing and sneezing soon spread disease to everyone in the crowded, airless room. Lung diseases meant that most men were crippled by their forties, and died shortly afterwards. Today the Pennine air is clean, fresh and healthy, but a hundred years ago lead miners there could expect to live even shorter lives than the crowded people of the worst Victorian slums in the big cities.

Thanks to the skills of industrial archaeologists, the great water-wheel at Killhope is turning once again. Site Director Ian Forbes at Killhope.

For younger readers:

History in Evidence: *Prehistoric Britain* Wayland
The Avebury Monuments Lawrence Coupland, English
Heritage
History in Evidence: *Saxon Britain* Wayland
In the Batsford series *How it Was*:
The Romans in Britain Dorothy Metcalf
Knights and Castles Madeline Jones
Tudor Monarchs Jessica Saraga
Elizabethan Life Stewart Ross
Workshop of the World Andrew Lee

For older readers:

English Heritage and Batsford jointly publish a series of
books giving accessible introductions to Britain's
archaeological heritage. The following are related to
topics in this book:
Avebury Caroline Malone
Stonehenge Julian Richards
Flag Fen Francis Pryor
Maiden Castle Niall Sharples
Hadrian's Wall Stephen Johnson
Roman Towns in Britain Guy de la Bédoyère
Anglo-Saxon England Martin Welch
Abbeys and Priories Glyn Coppack

A summary of four thousand years of Britain's history is
given by Andrew Hayes in *Archaeology of the British
Isles* (Batsford), and a very good introduction to
archaeological practice and theory can be found in *The
Amateur Archaeologist* by Stephen Wass (Batsford).
    English Heritage produce guides to all the properties in
their care. The Welsh caves of the Stone Age are described
in *Ice Age Hunters* by Stephen Green; archaeological
sites of Orkney are included in *Scotland BC* by Anna
Ritchie (Historic Scotland).

Places to visit:

Orkney: Historic Scotland. Skara Brae, Barnhouse, Maes
Howe, the Stones of Stenness and the Ring of Brodgar.
Avebury: National Trust/English Heritage. This site is in
Wiltshire, 16km south of Swindon. Access at any
reasonable time. The Alexander Keiller Museum (06723
250) has displays of objects from Avebury and Windmill
Hill. Windmill Hill, West Kennet long barrow, The
Sanctuary and Silbury Hill can also be visited.

Flag Fen: This is on the outskirts of Peterborough and has
a visitor centre with displays of objects from the site.
There are also guided tours of the excavations (Tel. no.
0733 313414).
Maiden Castle: English Heritage. The hillfort is just to
the south of the town of Dorchester in Dorset. Access at
any reasonable time. There are display boards around the
site giving information. Some of the objects found at
Maiden Castle are in the County Museum in Dorchester.
Birdoswald: English Heritage/Cumbria County Council.
Here there are the remains of a fort and substantial
stretches of the Wall are visible. There is also a visitor
centre with displays (Tel. no. 06977 47602).
Cosmeston: Near Penarth in South Wales (off the
B4267). Within a country park the deserted medieval
village has been reconstructed and can be visited by
guided tours. Open daily (Tel. no. 0222 701678).
Southampton: English Heritage has recently restored a
medieval merchant's house at 58 French Street.
Battle: English Heritage. In Sussex, the site of the battle
and the ruins of the Abbey are visible.
Kirby Hall: Near Corby in Northamptonshire. It is in the
care of English Heritage, who are reconstructing the
gardens (Tel. no. 0536 203230).
Killhope: At Killhope visitors have the opportunity to try
their hand at some of the tasks. There is a visitor centre
and shop. Invalid access. Parties should book (Tel. no.
0388 537505).

Acknowledgements

This book is based on the BBC Children's Television
series *Now Then*, first broadcast in 1990 (First Series)
and 1991 (Second Series). The programmes were devised
and produced by David Collison for Third Eye
Productions Ltd; they were written and directed by
Roderick Graham. The archaeological consultant and
presenter of the first series was the late Tony Gregory; the
second series was presented by Francis Pryor. Paul
Birkbeck drew the illustrations and appeared as the Artist
in both series. The photographs are by David Collison.
Mr Birkbeck's illustrations are reproduced with the kind
permission of BBC Children's Television (copyright
reserved); the two Maiden Castle reconstructions are
copyright English Heritage. The Time Children's
costumes were by Mary Charlton and the replica objects
by Bim Hopewell, both of Heritage Projects Ltd. Music
for the series was by Graeme and Wendy Lawson
(Archaeologia Musica).